16

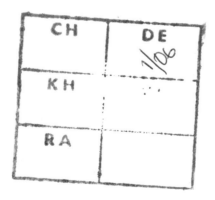

the **Persian cat**

A guide to selection, care, nutrition,
behaviour, breeding and health

Content

Foreword

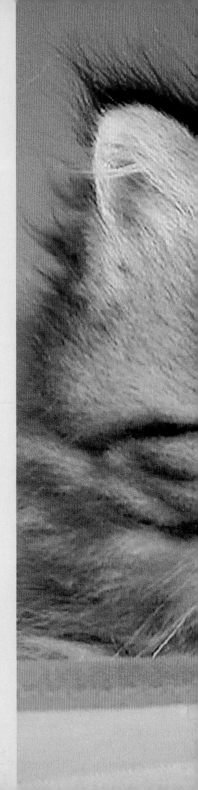

The book you have in your hands does not claim to be a complete book about the Persian cat. If we had collected all the information about the breed, its history, development, feeding, care, health, illnesses and everything else there is to know, this book would have to consist of at least three hundred pages.

What we have done, however, is to gather all the basic information that you, as the (future) owner of a Persian, need to know in order to handle your pet responsibly. Unfortunately, it seems that there are still a lot of people who buy a pet before really knowing what they are about to get into.

This book basically deals with the history of the Persian, the breed standard and the advantages and disadvantages of keeping cats. There is also essential information about feeding your cat and an introduction to breeding. Finally, day-to-day care, health and breed-specific ailments are also dealt with.

After having read this book, you can make the well-considered decision to buy a Persian and keep it as a pet in a responsible manner. We advise you, however, not to leave it at just this book. There are excellent books available that go deeper into certain topics, for which we do not have the space in this small book.

About Pets

about pets

A Publication of About Pets.

Copyright © 2003
About Pets
co-publisher United Kingdom
Kingdom Books
PO9 5TL, England

ISBN 185279240X
First printing
December 2004

Original title: *de Perzisch langhaar*
© 2004 Welzo Media Productions bv,
Warffum, the Netherlands
www.aboutpets.info

Photos: Anneke Burry,
Ron and Inca van Garderen,,
Rob Dekker and Gerda Ras

Editor: Anneke Tasseron

Printed in China
through Printworks Int. Ltd.

In general

The first catlike creatures appeared in the order of carnivores in the Eocene, approximately 47 million years ago. The fossilised finds of these catlikes date from the Oligocene, approximately 37 million years ago.

Bi-colour, blue with white

These animals evolved quickly, and only about a million years ago, a cat similar to the leopard lived in North America. This *Miracinonyx trumani* became extinct approximately 10,000 years ago. The sabre-toothed tiger (also known as sabre-toothed cat) is a more famous catlike animal, which also died out 10,000 years ago.

In molecular genetics, use is made of the DNA. By figuring out how many mutations could have occurred in a certain space of time, scientists can make a quantitative estimation about when species evolved. The first branch of carnivores developed approximately 12 million years ago, in the Miocene, and it lead to the development of, among others, the Margay, the Ocelot and the

American Tiger Cat (which lives in forests). Two to four million years later, the wild cats followed with the Jungle Cat and the Manul (which lives in savannahs). These are very closely related to our domestic cat.

Research has revealed that our domestic cat is a direct descendant of the African Wildcat (*Felis silvestris lybica*). The very first domesticated cats were those of the ancient Egyptians. They revered the cat as a divine being. Whether domesticating the cat was based on religious motives is not clear. The cat also had a very important function in protecting the harvest, as it caught mice. Maybe both these functions of the cat were intertwined, and the protection of the grain through the cat was seen as divine intervention. The Egyptians declared cats as holy creatures: killing a cat was severely punished, and exporting them was also prohibited. Trade routes, though, eventually brought the cat to China, further into the Middle East and to Europe.

It is not quite clear when cats were domesticated. Some excavations prove that contact – or a form of cohabitation with humans – has existed for some while. Excavations were made in Jericho, for example, where 9000 year old remains were found. The finds of mummified cats in Egypt are known worldwide. Images of cats can also be found on Egyptian tomb paintings. Cat worship was at its height in Egypt approximately 3500 years ago.

History

The history of the Persian cat is not easy to trace. This is because of the breed's very long breeding history. Little or nothing was recorded of the starting period. The long list of different coat and eye colours is proof of the Persian's long history as a pedigree cat. At the beginning, the Persian only existed in self (single) colours – crossing in the point-gene produced the colourpoints. The Persian kept its typical coat throughout all the breeding programmes: it is the only real longhaired cat that we know. Other cats with fairly long hair are called semi-longhaired cats.

Plenty of often strange theories have been created about the development of pedigree cats. More often than not, however, these theories can be proven to be false - at least as far as science is concerned.
According to such theories, the Persian is a descendant of the Pallas' Cat (*Felis manul*). However much this cat might look longhaired, however, it is genetically shorthaired. There are also plenty of variations on the same theme, presenting all sorts of possible mixtures with the Pallas' Cat.

Other people looked towards Russia on their search, as they believed that the Persian might have developed from mixes with longhaired Russian cats. The Persian might also be a descendant of the Siberian Forest Cat.
This last theory does make some sense, as having a long coat is more useful in a cold habitat (Siberia) than in Persia.

The development of a long coat in a warm country cannot be dismissed totally, however. Every species, both in fauna and flora, has its own genetic niche. Species evolve: each species has become adapted to its habitat with time.

The development of novelties, such as a long coat, curled ears, a curly coat or short legs, is caused

Bluepoint

Bi-colour, blue with white

by a mutation of the genome. Whether or not such a mutation is beneficial for a species' future depends on the circumstances. If it is a disadvantage to the species, then individuals with this mutation will cease to exist after a few generations. To put it in other words: the Persian cat's long coat could have developed in the Middle East after all.

The Italian Pietro della Valle is the first person to describe the Persian, and probably also the first one to give this cat the name 'Persian'. A travel account of Pietro della Valle appeared in the "Historie naturelle, générale et particulière" by Georg Louis Leclerc de Buffus. In this, the Persian is described as a bluish grey cat with a lighter undercoat and a long, fine, shiny overcoat, which curls slightly on the chest and the belly. It has a longhaired tail, which is carried curled over its back. Pietro della Valle had cats from Persia imported to his home country, but it is impossible to find out what happened to his breeding plans.

Another longhaired cat was already known in Europe: the Turkish Angora. This was very quickly pushed aside by the Persian in cat shows in Great Britain, although Frances Simpson, an expert, wrote in 1903 that the differences between these breeds were merely subtle. Over the past century,

the breed has more and more developed its own characteristics and we can now admire some stunningly beautiful Persians.

Standard of Points
Standards of points have been written for all cat breeds. With newly bred or mutated breeds, the standard is usually written in the country of origin and later translated into other languages, usually by the breed association of that country. A standard of points is sometimes subject to changes even after it has been published, and not all associations and countries have the same standard.

A standard is a point of reference for breeders and judges. It describes an ideal, which each cat of the breed should fulfil. With some breeds, cats are already being bred that fulfil the ideal, whereas other breeds still have a long way to go. For each breed, a list with defects has been established. These can be severe faults, which lead to a cat being excluded from breeding. Permissible faults are less severe, but will cost points at shows. You will be able to obtain the different standards from the relevant associations.

Standard of Points for the Persian
The Persian should be a solid balanced cat with a massive head in proportion to its body which should be short and cobby with

broad chest, sturdy legs, large paws and a short full tail. The cat should have a long flowing coat.

Head and Ears - Head round and massive with great breadth of skull; well balanced. Small round-tipped ears, set wide apart and low on the head, fitting into the rounded contour of the head, with ear furnishings but not unduly open at the base. Full cheeks; round forehead.
Short broad nose of even width with stop (break). Nose leather fully formed.
Strong chin and full muzzle with broad powerful jaws, without a 'pinch'. Short thick neck.

Eyes - Large full round eyes; brilliant in colour and set well apart. Bold and not deep set.

Body - Large or medium in size; of cobby type; low on the legs. Broad deep chest; massive shoulders and rump; well muscled.

Legs and Paws - Short thick strong legs. Large round firm paws; preferably well tufted. Toes carried close; five in front and four behind.

Tail - Short and bushy but in proportion to body length.

Coat - Long and thick. Fine in texture; not excessively woolly. Soft and full of life. Full frill covering

Scale of Points

Head	25	including general shape of head, forehead; set of eyes; shape and set of ears; nose length; width and stop; width of cheeks and muzzle; chin
Eyes	15	including size, shape and colour
Body	20	including shape, size and bone structure, tail and length of tail, height, thickness of legs and paws
Coat	40	including colour texture and quality; evenness of colour
Total	**100**	**points**

the shoulders and continuing into a deep frill between the front legs. Cats should be shown in good general condition and well presented.

Faults are: a bent tail, teeth not closing properly due to an under-shot or an overshot jaw, an eye colour that is not permitted with the cat's coat colour.

Coat colours and patterns
The number of possible combinations of colours with different patterns adds up to a few hundred. This is obviously too much to be dealt with here. It is, however, interesting to note the increase in colours during the last century.

The blue Persian, as it is seen in the description by Judge John Jennings from 1893, was the standard at the beginning. These cats were even popular with Queen Victoria. Although the black Persian was known before,

White

it was not until 1890 that the first black Persian cat appeared at a show in Great Britain.

As genetics was not very far advanced yet, only male red cats were recognised to start with. It was not yet clear how one could breed red females. In this period, around 1915, the first crème Persians also entered the scene. Blue developed from black under the influence of the gene responsible for colour dilution. This gene was very common among Persians. This also explains why crème Persians appeared soon after red Persians were crossed in. The gene that diluted black to blue also diluted red to crème. The white Persian was only accepted with blue eyes until 1938. The orange-eyed and the odd-eyed (eyes of two different colours) have, however, also been recognised for some time now.

Persians with tabby patterns have also become increasingly popular. The American judge Mr. Barker was offered 1000 dollars for his Persian, which he imported from England. Princess Victoria of Schleswig-Holstein also bred silver tabby Persians.
The silvers made quite an entrance. Chinchilla, shaded silver and smoke are the varieties of silver which are particularly beautiful on the Persian's long coat. The smoke Persian appeared at a show as early as 1893.

From a genetic point of view, the development of the black tortoiseshell (and the blue tortoiseshell / with white) was a logical progression from the recognition of red and crème tomcats in 1928. But at the beginning of the 20th century, genetics was not yet this far advanced. Breeding with tortoiseshell tomcats was also unsuccessful, i.e. no kittens were produced. Today, it is known that, due to a chromosome abnormality, tortoiseshell tomcats are sterile.

Nora Woodifield, a British breeder, was the person to start breeding Persians with piebald spotting.

The Dutch breeder Karl Tjebbes crossed in the Siamese to establish the point markings in Persians too. In Britain and America, breeders were experimenting with similar crossings. Only in 1955, however, the GCCP recognised Persians with pointed markings, which have become known as colourpoints. The colourpoint bred in America is primarily known as Himalayan and was recognised as an independent breed in 1957. Only in the 80s did the CFA add the Himalayan as a colourpoint to the Persian population. A nice side effect of the addition of the point-gene is that other colour genes came with it, such as chocolate and lilac. These last colours were recognised in the 70s.

Buying your Persian

Once you have made that well-considered decision to buy a cat and have chosen the Persian as your ideal breed, there are several ways you can proceed. Would you prefer a kitten or a grown cat, a female cat or a tomcat? Should it be a pedigree cat or a cross, or could it even be a cat from an animal shelter?

The question will naturally also arise as to where to buy your Persian. Will you get it from an individual, a reliable breeder or would you maybe even like to get a loveable Persian from an animal shelter? It is important for you and the animal that you sort out any such questions in advance. You want a cat that suits your lifestyle, so that you can offer it a good home. If you buy a kitten, you will have a playful, energetic housemate, which will easily adapt to its new surroundings. If you prefer things a little quieter, an adult or even an older cat would be a good choice.

Pros and cons of the Persian

A big advantage of buying a cat is that it can basically entertain itself. A cat really enjoys the presence of its owner, but if circumstances demand that you spend a weekend away from home

you can quite easily leave your Persian alone with a clear conscience, as long as you provide it with a clean litter box and plenty of water and food (you should get a food dispenser with a timer, which you can buy at a pet shop). Do this only if absolutely necessary, however! It would be preferable, of course, if a friendly neighbour or a friend could come to check on the cat and give it some company.

A cat will make your home a lot cosier. A Persian is quite capable of entertaining itself, but it will come to its master quite regularly. It will also come to you to remind you when it is feeding time. Your cat does not really have a master, but rather cohabitates with you. A lot of Persians are really cuddly, but some prefer to be left alone.

Cats are very clean animals, and your Persian will take care of quite a lot of its 'personal hygiene' itself. A true longhaired cat, such as the Persian, does, however, need to be combed approximately once or twice a week. Combing removes tangles, dead hair and other things, such as twigs, from your cat's fur. When taking care of its coat, you should also check your pet for any parasites, such as fleas. Many cats think that all the attention they are given during their grooming sessions is very interesting and will cooperate quite happily. The question is whether you are sure that you can take care of your Persian's coat with the necessary regularity.

As far as upkeep and vet's bills are concerned, a cat is not really an expensive pet. The average Persian is not very big even when fully grown, and is thus not a big eater. An annual vaccination is sufficient, and it is advisable to have a full health-check done at the same time.

Keeping a cat does, however, have some disadvantages, which you need to be aware of when deciding whether to buy one. Sharp nails are of vital importance to a cat. It has to be able to quickly climb up trees if danger is approaching, and it also needs its claws to hunt and to defend its territory. Your cat will therefore need a place to sharpen its nails, even if it is kept indoors. Cats will generally use a scratching pole or plank for this purpose, but you can also allow it to use an old chair. Your

cat will normally understand that it is to use this chair only, and leave the rest of your furniture in peace.

The Persian is a cat that is easy to keep as a pet, but if you cannot live with cat hair all over the furniture, or with an animal that instinctively needs to sharpen its nails – and might use your furniture to do this – then you should better not buy a cat at all. There will be times when you need to care for your Persian's coat on a daily basis, such as in the spring, when the winter coat is changed for the summer coat and extra grooming sessions will be advisable. The Persian is not an obtrusive cat, and it can quite happily be kept indoors only. Do not get too many cats if you do not have much space or if you are very busy: the more Persians, the more time you need to invest in caring for their coats.

Male or female?

Whether you want a male or a female cat is an entirely personal decision. A castrated tomcat generally has a very even-tempered nature, because he is not subject to hormonal changes like a (non-sterilised) female. A female cat can be quite moody due to her – regularly re-occurring – season. Most members of the cat family (lions, for example, are an exception here) do not live in groups in the wild, but prefer to live a solitary life. It is impossible to tell whether a tomcat or a female cat is more pleasant to handle day to day. An adult tomcat is generally bigger than an adult

Seal point

female. Persian tomcats are like big, good-natured teddy bears, whereas females are often a lot more resourceful.

The decision for a male or a female is normally determined by any plans you might have for your future pet. If you might want to breed a litter at some stage, it obviously makes sense to get a female. People who just want a companion quite often choose a tomcat, as they often look nicer when they are fully grown. Castrating a tomcat is a lot cheaper, but also a lot less invasive, than sterilising a female. Other people choose a female cat, as they are worried about a male 'spraying'. When spraying the tomcat marks his territory by urinating against objects. Female cats can also display this behaviour, however. It is then usually the sign of an approaching season. If you intend to buy a cat as a pet, and don't want to use it to breed, then you can naturally choose either a tomcat or a female cat.

The female cat

As far as general care is concerned, there is little difference between female and male cats. When female cats become sexually mature, they go 'on heat' or come 'in season'. The heat will normally return every three weeks, and this is the fertile period, when a female cat can become pregnant. If you do not keep your female together with a male, she will do her best to escape through the front door when you are not paying attention, or climb through an open window, in order to find a partner for mating. A female on heat definitely knows how to make herself heard.

Tortoiseshell blue-cream and creamtabby point

She will do this not only during the day, but also in the evenings and at night, when you really want to sleep. A lot of people think that their female cat is in agony when she comes in season for the first time. You would not be the first owner to go and consult a vet with your on-heat cat. Besides her loud and mournful crying, the female will also rub her head against anything and anyone she comes across. If she is really seriously on heat, she will go down with her front legs, and lift her genital area up whilst holding her tail to the side. Every (loose) tomcat in the area will respond to her calls and come to urinate against your door, just to announce his presence.

Female cats are generally sterilised when they are approximately ten months old. If a female develops quickly, she can come into her first, adolescent, season when she is only six months old. A disadvantage of having a female cat sterilised is that it involves abdominal surgery and therefore is a lot more invasive and expensive than having a tomcat castrated.

The tomcat

Generally, a tomcat is the easiest choice. As long as he is castrated at about ten months old.
When a tomcat becomes sexually mature, he may start spraying. He will mark his territory with urine. He may spray against your three-piece suite, the dining table legs, long curtains, the fridge, etc. This very penetrating smell is not always easy to remove from all materials.

If your tomcat does spray, a castration will normally solve this problem. In some cases, the cat will carry on spraying, or even start to do so, after a castration. Spraying is purely instinctive in tomcats before castration, whereas it is believed that spraying that starts after castration is taught behaviour, because the hormonal control is disrupted. A hormonal treatment may, however, solve the problem. Homeopathic remedies can also produce excellent results. An advantage of having a tomcat castrated is that it is a lot less invasive and also a lot less expensive than having a female cat sterilised.

Kitten or adult cat?

After choosing between male and female, you now have to make the next decision, i.e. whether you want a kitten or an adult cat. Some people believe that a kitten still needs to learn to do its business in the litter box. This is, however, wrong, as its mother will have taught the kitten to use the litter box from when it was about four weeks old. You can assume that an adult cat will be house-trained.

A kitten requires a lot more work than an adult cat. A kitten likes to play and loves to experience all (im)possibilities of life. It will need extra attention to get it accustomed to people and possibly other pets.

A general assumption about cats is that you can teach them to do things, but never not to do things. It is difficult to train a cat – both kitten and adult – not to do something. What will normally help, however, is to attract your cat's attention when it is planning something dangerous (such as going for the electric wiring, which kittens often want to bite into). If you call your kitten's name in such a situation, it will come to you and will forget what it was about to do.

An adult cat will, hopefully, no longer attempt to do naughty or dangerous things. Older animals often find forbidden things far less interesting, while kittens feel challenged by everything and anything. A kitten will cause a good deal of mayhem in its first few months. Curtains make interesting scratching devices, a plant makes brilliant prey, and a three-piece suite may also get far too much attention from your kitten. You cannot really teach a cat how to behave, as you can with a dog. It is important to keep a close eye on your cat, so that you can correct it when it enters forbidden territory or attempts dangerous undertakings. Finally, financial aspects might also influence whether you choose an adult cat or a kitten. A kitten is generally more expensive than an adult cat.

Looking after a kitten also requires a lot more time than looking after an adult cat. A kitten will constantly want to play, whereas an adult cat will often be a lot calmer. On the other hand, an adult cat will need more time to get used to its new home and its new housemate(s). A kitten's inquisitive nature will often win over its instinctive fear. A good way to socialise your kitten is to cuddle it a lot and play with it, thus giving it plenty of attention.

Both a kitten and an adult cat will require some of your time and energy. Get advice from a breeder. Maybe you have other pets, and then you will need to consider those too. An older, not too sociable, cat is more likely to tolerate a kitten than another adult cat in its territory. The Persian will try to avoid conflicts, and it is also tolerant towards other pets.

Two cats?

Having two or more cats in the house at the same time is not just more fun for you, but also for your cats. Cats can derive a lot of pleasure out of the company of their own kind. They can clean each other's coats and play with each other.

The combination of male and female needs extra attention, and it is not a good idea to get a male and a female kitten from the same litter. It is advisable to choose two kittens of the same sex, as this prevents a lot of problems. If a female cat is covered too young, she will not be able to carry out the young (resulting in premature birth) or, if the pregnancy goes well, she might not be able to look after the young afterwards. Tomcats can mate from the age of approximately six months (they are usually a little older, but it can happen this early).

If you are sure that you want two young cats, you need to decide whether you want to get them at the same time, or whether you want to give it some time before buying the second cat. Cats are more vulnerable to viruses than dogs, for example. If you buy two kittens from different catteries and one of them is/becomes ill, it is often impossible to tell where the illness came from (the one cat might have a stronger resistance than the other). Buying two kittens from the same cattery can therefore prevent problems with breeders. Moving home is very stressful for cats and a stressed cat is more receptive to disease.

Two grown cats can quite easily be brought into your home together, especially if they already know each other. If that is not the case, you need to let them get to know each other.

Cats and children

Persians get on very well with children. They can play together and have a lot of fun with each other, and your children will also learn to handle living beings. They develop a sense of responsibility by looking after a cat (or another pet).

However cute a cat might be, children need to learn that it is a living being and not a cuddly toy. A cat does not feel comfortable if it is being messed around with. If a kitten is pestered a lot by children, it is hardly surprising if it becomes less attached to humans or even becomes scared. If a cat feels

Silver tabby

Red tabby point

Blue point

Black tabby with white

Blue

uncomfortable, it will usually give a short, yet clear, warning by striking out with its paw, usually with its claws extended. If a frightened child (or adult) pulls its hand back, it will look as if the cat was scratching the person. A cat will strike out when something is happening to it that it does not like. Make it clear to children what a cat likes and what it doesn't. Also show the child how it can play with the cat. Rolling a ball can be great fun, as cats will generally run after it. The child can also throw a few bits of dry food for the cat to chase after instead of a ball. The cat will run after the food, eat it and come back for the next round. Children also have to learn to leave a cat in peace when it doesn't want to play any more. The cat needs to have its own place it can withdraw to when it wants to be undisturbed. Have your children help as much as possible with your cat's care. This will result in a strong bond and child and animal will learn to trust and deal with each other.

The arrival of a baby also means changes to your cat's life. If the nursery is to be a prohibited area for the cat once the baby is born, prevent your cat entering it from the very beginning. Never leave a cat alone with small children. Normally, not much will happen, as a cat will make sure that it escapes in time if it feels uncomfortable in a certain situation. There is more of a danger to the child if the cat knocks things over when fleeing, as these objects could hit a crawling infant.

Infants are very inquisitive. They will try to see whether the cat's tail comes off, or whether its eyes come out, just as they do with their cuddly toys. Being pulled at the tail causes a cat a lot of pain! Keep a close watch on your cat and child(ren), as accidents can lurk anywhere!

Cats and dogs

Despite the fact that their body talk is a lot different, Persians and dogs can get along a lot better than many people assume. If a dog lies on its back, it is a sign of submission. If a cat lies on its back, it is by no means a sign of submission, but it means that the cat has its best weapon, i.e. its claws, at its disposal. Cats and dogs do, however, have one important thing in common: if the other goes too far, they both growl, and both species understand this!

Where nutrition is concerned, a dog and cat should not eat each other's food. If a cat is fed on dog food only, it can start vomiting quite badly. Eating from one bowl is a no-no too. A dog does not like sharing its food. It will quickly show an overconfident kitten its limits. It is fine for your cat and dog to play together, but you must not let them eat together.

Some dogs think that chasing cats is great fun. You have to prohibit this behaviour from the very start, as cats also have their rights! Cats, on the other hand, sometimes like to torment dogs. If this is the case, it is best to let the animals sort out their conflict amongst themselves. A dog is very capable of learning that a cat is not a toy. To prevent nastier fights in the future, you should correct your dog and chase your cat away. If a cat is in a real state of panic, it is advisable not to pick it up, but to let it quietly calm down again on its own.

Where to buy your Persian
There are different ways of acquiring a cat. Whether you want a kitten or an adult cat will normally determine where to buy your cat.

If it is to be a kitten, you need to find a breeder with a litter. Breed clubs normally have very good kitten agencies. If you choose a popular breed, such as the Persian, you will have plenty of choice. You might, however, encounter the problem that there are some kittens for sale that have only been bred for profit's sake. Those breeders do not look out for breed-specific ailments and in-breeding. The kittens are also taken away from their mother as quickly as possible, and are thus insufficiently socialised. Some countries have made it a law that kittens are to remain with their mothers for at least seven weeks. Cat breed associations make it obligatory for their members not to give away their kittens before they have been vaccinated completely. This might mean that you can only pick up your kitten when it is thirteen to sixteen weeks old; in some cases you might even have to wait seventeen weeks.

There are, fortunately, plenty of bona-fide breeders of Persian cats. Try and visit several breeders before buying your kitten. Also ask the breeder whether he'll be willing to help you find solutions to any problems that you might encounter after having bought your kitten.

There is one place where you should never be tempted to take home a kitten: at a cat show. The day was already stressful enough for the animal. Viruses and bacteria can easily be transmitted at shows, and the kitten might become ill when you have brought it home. If you see a kitten you like at a show, make an appointment to visit the breeder's home, for example for the weekend after the show. A serious breeder will not have a problem to reserve the kitten for you until then.

Red classic tabby

You also need to realise that a pedigree is nothing more or less than a proof of descent. The breed associations also issue pedigrees for kittens whose parents were suffering from hereditary ailments, or have not been checked for them. A pedigree therefore says nothing about the animals used for breeding.

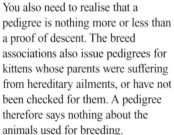
Blue tabby

If you plan to buy an adult cat, you can contact a breed association or a cat club. They can also give you some phone numbers where you can get more information on cats looking for a new home. A breed association will also know of grown cats that need to be re-homed due to their owners' circumstances (e.g. impulse buying, moving home, divorce).

Things to watch out for

Buying a kitten is not to be taken too lightly. You especially need to be aware of the following:

• Never buy a cat on impulse, even if it is love at first sight. A cat is a living being, which needs a lot of care and attention for a long time (10 to 15 years, or even longer). It is not a toy that you can put away when you've finished with it.

• Take a good look at the mother cat. Is she happy, well cared for or neglected? The mother's behaviour and condition is not only an indication of the quality of the breeder, but also of the kitten you are about to buy.

• Do not buy a kitten whose mother was only kept in a cage or a separate room. A kitten needs to get as many impressions as possible during the first few weeks of its life, including living in a family. This way it gets used to people and other animals. Otherwise you might end up with a very shy cat rather than the cuddly, sociable 'lap cat' you always wanted.

• Always ask to see the parents' papers (vaccination certificates, pedigrees, official results of health examinations).

• Never buy a kitten that is younger than twelve weeks.

• Make all agreements with the breeder in writing.

Tortoiseshell cat, blue cream white

Moving to a new home

Once you have found the Persian of your dreams, you will have to start making some preparations. The animal is about to undergo the most stressful experience of its life, so you should make sure that everything goes smoothly.

White

Shoppinglist
Water bowl
Food bowl
Litter box
Cat litter
Cat litter scoop
Dry food
Canned food
Comb
Brush
Scratching pole
Toys
Transport basket

The preparations

If you have chosen a kitten or even an adult cat at a breeder's, then you will usually be given a list of the food and the cat litter that the animal is used to.
It is advisable to feed your cat the same food that it was fed at the breeder's, at least at the beginning. A too abrupt change of food can easily lead to diarrhoea with cats. It is also best to stick to the breeder's feeding times at the beginning. If you got your cat from an animal shelter and you don't know much about its past, then you need to be creative and try out which food your new companion likes best and which cat litter it prefers.

Once you have got all the information you need, you can go to a pet shop and buy all the

necessary equipment. Do this in plenty of time. Don't pick up your kitten first and then hurry to the pet shop. Your kitten will have already soiled a corner of the room before you had time to unpack, and it will also feel uncomfortable with all the stress around it.

Picking up your cat

Make very clear arrangements with the other party. Find out the shelter's opening times. And stick to your appointment. Breeders are individuals, not shops. Make sure that you have the right amount of money with you, and don't start bargaining; you are not on a cattle market! Ask any questions that you might have concerning your kitten's well-being. Take your time for this, the breeder will appreciate your concerns. Do not, however,

stay until dinner. A cattery is not a restaurant!

Keep an eye on the weather. You probably made your appointment weeks ago, and it could suddenly be 30 degrees on the day you want to pick up your kitten. Plan your trip early in the morning. The temperature can rise quite quickly in a car. If you cannot avoid driving in the heat, put a wet towel over the transport basket.

If you sometimes take your dog in the car, then you might have fleas in it. Before picking up your kitten, spray the car well with a good anti-flea spray. Otherwise your negligence will make it seem as if your new housemate is a flea-store.

You can take food and water for the kitten with you, but there is not normally much point in this. Cats do not enjoy travelling and your kitten will almost certainly not want to drink or eat. If you have to travel a long distance and it is hot, then take a pipette with you, so that you can drip some water into your kitten's mouth once in a while.

The first few days

Once you have arrived at home with your new housemate, you will have a few busy days awaiting you. Your kitten needs to learn where its litter box is. Don't place it too far away from the living room, as it will probably have to get to it quite quickly at the beginning. Also show it where its food and drink bowls are.

Most kittens really miss their mother and siblings. Sometimes, a kitten will hide under a cupboard (when you are in the room), and you won't get to see it for a few days. Walking around and meowing loudly are also quite normal at this stage. If you answer your kitten's meowing by calling its name, it will soon get to know its name and come to you. Your kitten will definitely make itself heard in this time of uncertainty.

Other pets

If you already have another (older) cat, you need to give the animals time to get used to each other. To start with, leave your

If you already had a cat before, you will be aware of the situations a kitten can end up in thanks to its adventurous nature. If this is your first cat, then you will soon notice that electricity cables are not safe from your kitten, that books can be pushed out of the book case, or that your beautiful house plant will be missing its leaves when you return from the kitchen, to name just a few examples. Be patient. Living with a cat means living with a very self-willed animal.

Problems and solutions

For people who already had cats before, the most obvious problems will be quite easy to solve. However, cats can always challenge their owners in totally new ways.

kitten alone in the living room for a while. This way, it can get used to its surroundings and find a safe hiding place in case it feels threatened by the other cat. Let the animals sort out the hierarchy amongst themselves. If you constantly intervene, it is difficult for the animals to size each other up.

Many sounds are the same in all households, but each house also has its very own noises. Your kitten might not have had a problem with the vacuum cleaner at the breeder's. Your vacuum cleaner might, however, sound totally different and therefore be very frightening. Other sounds around it might also scare your kitten and make it hide in a safe place.

Your kitten does not listen to its name: once in a while, the animal will meow – sometimes quite pitifully – to call its mother and siblings. "Answer" these calls by calling its name in a cheerful manner.

Your kitten scuttles along the skirting boards and meows in a pitiful manner: it got lost and is actually looking for the litter box. Gently pick it up and patiently set it down in the litter box.

Your kitten does its business next to the litter box: A young animal needs to get used to rather a lot in a new environment. You can try moving the litter box to the spot your kitten has chosen to do its business. Prevention is better: place the litter box near the spot where your kitten came out of its travel basket and where it tends to play most. The litter box can easily be too far away for a young kitten.

Calling for food and then not eating: This should not normally happen if the previous owner or breeder gave you a correct list. This is more common with cats "without a past". Your cat is probably really hungry, but "its" food is not there. Try another tin of a different brand. If this happens on a Sunday, cook a fish fillet to have food until the beginning of the week. If this problem occurs with dry food, ask the pet store for some trial-size packets.

Not wanting to eat: This problem is more common with young and adult cats than with kittens. Most of the time – if the problem appears during the first few days – the reason is homesickness. A cat that refuses to eat for a week will suffer Hepatic Lipidosis (a serious liver condition) and can die as a result of this. If a cat refuses its food for more than two or three days, it needs to be force-fed.

Your kitten suffers from diarrhoea within the first few days in its new home: This is usually caused by changes in feeding. Give your kitten the food it was fed at the breeder's. If you did this, try to remember whether you let your cat lick out empty custard or yoghurt tubs or fed it pieces of cheese or sausage. This too can be a serious change in your cat's diet, and can really upset its stomach and intestines.

Diarrhoea doesn't stop: A kitten can dehydrate very quickly and it will lose a lot of fluid when suffering from diarrhoea. If the breeder couldn't give you any advice that worked, go to your vet to be on the safe side.

Feeding your Persian

A cat is a typical carnivore. A wild cat will normally hunt small mammals, such as mice, but it will also not say no to the odd bird if it can catch it.

A cat will also eat its victim's innards and its stomach with the semi-digested plant material. In this way, it supplements its meat menu with the necessary vitamins and minerals. This is also the basis for feeding your domestic cat.

Cats have very sensitive intestines. Suddenly changing your cat's food can lead to serious diarrhoea. If you want to change your cat's diet, it is advisable to do it gradually by mixing slowly increasing proportions of the new food with the old food.

Ready-made food

It is not easy for a layman to put together a complete menu for a cat, which includes all the necessary proteins, fats, vitamins and minerals in just the right amounts and proportions. Meat is not a complete meal for your cat, as it contains too little calcium. A continuous calcium deficiency will eventually lead to bone problems (such as osteoporosis). If you mix your cat's food yourself, you are also likely to feed it too much in terms of vitamins and minerals. This can be just as bad for your cat's health as feeding too little!

You can prevent all these food-related problems by feeding your cat ready-made food of a good brand. These products are well balanced, and they contain everything your cat needs in terms of nutrition. Supplements (such as vitamin preparations) are superfluous. How much food your cat needs depends on its weight and activity level. You will find general guidelines on the packaging.

A lot of cats are fed dry food. A cat does not like eating big portions, and you can put enough dry food in the bowl for your cat to nibble at throughout the day. You also need to put a bowl with fresh drinking water next to your cat's food. If you feed your cat only canned food, it is best to spread it over two meals a day. If the cat does not eat its portion in one go, you can let it stand for a while if you know that your cat will eat it fairly soon. If it is a warm day, however, remains of canned food will attract flies, and they will lay their eggs in the food.

As its nutritional requirements depend, among other things, on a cat's age and lifestyle, there are all sorts of different types of food available. There are 'light' foods, special kitten foods, foods for cats kept indoors only, and senior foods for older cats.

Dry kitten food

There is currently a wide assortment of dry kitten food on the market. These foods contain an increased amount of growth-promoting nutrients, such as protein and calcium. Check on the packaging to see up to which age the manufacturer classes a cat as a 'kitten'. If you also have an older

cat, for example, which is being fed senior food, then you need to feed the two cats separately. However, it won't hurt your kitten to be fed food for adult cats once in a while.

Canned food or dry food?

Ready-made food, which you can buy in a supermarket or at a pet shop, can generally be divided into canned food (or food from a pouch), and dry food.

Most cats love canned food. There is, however, a major disadvantage: it is soft. A cat that is only fed canned food will sooner or later develop dental problems (plaque, paradontosis). Besides giving canned food, regularly feed your cat dry food. If your cat prefers to eat meat, try to change the brand and taste of its dry food once in a while. Curiosity will probably make your cat eat some of the dry food eventually.

As dry food has its water extracted, it is important that you provide your cat with fresh drinking water. The advantage of dry food is that it is quite hard, which forces the cat to use its jaws. When your cat chews its dry food, tartar is removed and the gums are massaged.

In-between treats

Of course, you want to spoil your cat with something extra once in a while. Do not feed your cat bits of

Dry food

Canned food

Small dried fish,
cats love them

Healthy treats

cheese or sausage, as they contain far too much salt and fat. A lot of people really want to spoil their cat and feed it cooked fish or fresh lamb's heart. Do not do this more often than once a week. There are plenty of special cat snacks and treats available in pet shops. If your cat has a tendency to become fat, deduct the treats from its daily amount of food.

The butcher's left-overs
Feeding your cat pork or poultry left-overs with bones attached to them is very dangerous. These bones can easily splinter and thus cause serious injury to your cat's intestines. Another waste-product from the butcher's is sheep's fat. This is an ideal food supplement if your cat is suffering from diarrhoea or weak intestines.

Fresh meat or fish
If you want to feed your cat fresh meat or fish once in a while, never feed it raw, but always boiled or roasted. Especially raw (or not fully cooked) pork can harbour the dangerous Aujeszky virus. There is no cure for this disease, and it will quickly lead to your pet's death. Raw chicken can be contaminated with the notorious Salmonella bacteria, but a cat is not susceptible to this. Cooked chicken (fillet) is often advised as a food when a cat is suffering from diarrhoea. Always wash your hands thoroughly after handling raw meat.

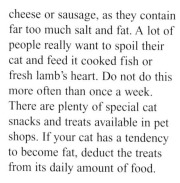

A lot of people think that cats are real fish-eaters. Apart from some catlike species, cats do not really catch fish. The fact that stray cats quite often hang around harbours is more due to the fact that it is easy to get food here, rather than them being mad about fish. If you want to feed your cat fish, you need to be aware that some species of fish should not be fed raw. Raw fish can contain thiaminasis, an enzyme that breaks down thiamine (aneurine or vitamin B1). Cats do not naturally have a supply of thiamine in their bodies, as they cannot produce it themselves. Thiamine is, however, a very important nutrient.

Drinking
Just as its nutritional requirements, a cat's need for water depends on environmental factors, such as the temperature, but also on the weight and activity level of the cat. Canned food contains a lot of water, whereas dry food has almost all of its water extracted. A cat fed on canned food will drink far less than a cat fed on dry food. A cat needs to have a bowl of fresh drinking water available all day long. Cats have difficulty digesting the lactose contained in cow's milk and therefore often suffer from diarrhoea after it. You can, however, buy special milk in pet shops, which has been modified for cats (cat milk).

Overweight?

Recent research has shown that a lot of cats in our country are overweight. A cat usually becomes overweight because it is fed too much food or too many treats between meals and because it plays too little (cats that are allowed outdoors will usually get more exercise). Greediness and boredom can also lead to a cat being overweight, as can castration and sterilisation. Due to the hormonal changes, the cat will become less active after surgery, and will use a lot less energy. Simply too little exercise will also lead to a cat becoming overweight. Not only a kitten enjoys a game, but a grown cat will also be thankful for some extra attention and play.

You can use the following rule of thumb to check if your cat is overweight: you need to be able to feel its ribs, but not see them. If you cannot feel your cat's ribs, then it is far too fat. Overweight cats live a passive life. They run and play a lot less and tire quite quickly. They are also more prone to illnesses and do not live as long.

It is important to prevent your cat becoming overweight. Always follow the guidelines on the feed packaging. Adapt it accordingly if your cat is less active or is fed a lot of snacks between meals. Also try to provide your cat with plenty

of exercise by playing with it a lot. If your cat is prone to becoming overweight, you need to give it food with fewer calories. If your cat is really too fat and adapting the amount of food does not help, you will have to put it on a special diet to make it lose weight. Ask your vet for advice in this matter.

Caring for your Persian

Good (day-to-day) care is important for your cat. A well cared-for cat is less likely to become ill.

Caring for your cat is not just an unavoidable necessity, but also a pleasure: owner and cat give each other all their attention. It is also a good time for a game and a cuddle.

The coat

The Persian needs intensive coat care due to the length of its coat. The coat can easily get tangled and knotted really badly if you do not intervene. Bad tangles 'pull' on the skin and eventually really hurt your cat. If the coat is knotted up right to the skin, then it might be necessary to have the animal clipped under anaesthetic at the vet's. Good coat care consists of regular brushing, combing and checking for parasites (such as fleas). Use the right equipment to take care of

your cat's coat. Combs must not be too sharp, and choose a brush made of natural hair.

Use a coarse comb for combing through the fur on the legs, the belly, back, breast and neck. Comb this hair against the direction it grows in. Use a fine comb for the shorter, finer hair on the face and behind the ears. To finish off, the whole coat is brushed over. A row brush adds volume to the coat. Try to pick out tangles, as pulling them out really hurts your cat.

If you get your kitten used to being combed and brushed at a young age, it will get to like having its coat cared for. Don't brush too long in one go, as kittens don't normally have the patience for extensive grooming sessions yet. If you very subtly increase the length of its grooming sessions, your kitten will get used to them without really noticing any change.

A Persian will need to have a bath once in a while, for example if it comes home dirty or if some chemical fluid has spilled on it by accident. If the latter is the case, also contact your vet. It is not easy to wash a cat. Some individuals and some breeds might 'like' water, but generally cats are not very keen on it. If your cat is not used to being bathed, it is advisable to ask another person for help. Here too,

your motto should be: 'Start 'em young'! Breeders generally let kittens get used to all the aspects of coat care. If you continue this training, your Persian will be easy to keep beautiful.

If you want to bathe your cat because it needs to go to a show, for example, its coat needs to be thoroughly combed and free of tangles before you make it wet. Irregularities and tangles are difficult to remove from a wet coat. Always use special cat shampoo. Make sure that no shampoo can get into the ears and eyes and rinse out any suds well. If your Persian kitten has been

Silver classic tabby

Make sure that you check your cat's fur right to the skin for any parasites or bald patches that might indicate fungi. Coat problems can also be the result of allergies to certain feed ingredients. Symptoms of this type of allergy are excessive scratching (due to the itch), redness and inflammations. This can occur at any age. If your cat is suffering from a food-related allergy, your vet can prescribe a hypoallergenic diet. Food intolerance also causes diarrhoea. In this case, too, the cat will be prescribed a hypoallergenic diet.

Teeth

A cat has to be able to eat properly to stay in good condition, so it needs healthy teeth. Therefore, check your cat's teeth regularly. If you think that all is not well, contact your vet. Regular feeds of hard dry food will contribute to clean, healthy teeth.

introduced to the hairdryer, this will be very useful later. A cat can catch a cold very easily, so make sure that it is thoroughly dry again very quickly.

Your vet can give you some medicinal shampoos to treat some skin conditions. Always follow the instructions! To prevent skin and fur problems from developing, it is very important to fight fleas and fungi properly. You need to treat fungi and fleas not only on the cat itself, but also in its surroundings (see chapter "Parasites").

Regularly brushing your cat's teeth is also a good way of keeping them healthy. You can use a special toothbrush for cats. If you plan to regularly brush your cat's teeth, you should get it used to this as a kitten. Use special cat toothpaste, as those for humans are unhealthy for cats. It is by no means easy to get an adult cat to accept having its teeth brushed.

It is not yet common in this country to brush cats' teeth. It is worth giving it a go, but if your cat really refuses to cooperate, then just make sure that it eats plenty of dry food and don't stress it too much. Just make sure that it eats enough dry food. If your cat refuses to eat dry food, you need to regularly check its teeth for tartar. Your vet can give the cat a light anaesthetic and remove the tartar.

A cat loses its first teeth when it is approximately four months old. It can happen that old and new canine teeth end up next to each other. The permanent tooth will normally push out the first tooth, but keep a good eye on it anyway, as first teeth sometimes need to be removed by a vet.

Nails

A cat can put its claws in or out. When it is walking around, standing, sitting or lying, it will have pulled its claws in. If you hold onto a toe and press carefully on the nail, then it will come out. A cat likes to have sharp nails. It needs them to defend itself, but also to climb up trees if danger is approaching. A cat sharpens its nails by scratching.

If you regularly cut your cat's nails, then it won't hurt so much if it lashes out at you with its paw. However, the more you cut your cat's nails, the more it will do its best to sharpen them. As long as the cat uses its scratching pole or

plank, and ignores your furniture, it is fine. If, however, you cut your cat's nails to prevent it from scratching the furniture, then you are stimulating just this.

There are probably two situations where it is really advisable to cut your cat's nails. The first situation is when you are planning to take your cat to a show. At a show, your cat will be surrounded by all sorts of strange sounds and movements, which can make it very nervous. It then might perceive the judge, the steward, or even you, as a threat and lash out. If the cat has had its nails cut, the resulting wounds will be less severe and the blunt nail will not get caught in the victim's skin.

The other situation where you should cut your cat's nails is when you bring your female cat to a tomcat to be covered. After mating, the female will instinctively strike out at the male, and you definitely want to prevent your cat cutting the beautiful tomcat's ear in half. If you cut off the tips of the nails, then such nasty injuries won't happen. It is easiest to cut nails with special nail scissors from the pet shop. You have to be very careful not to cut the nail off too far, as you might hit the blood vessels, which can cause really unpleasant bleeding. If you are unsure about cutting your cat's nails yourself, have it done by a vet.

Cleaning your cat's eyes only takes a few seconds a day, so do it regularly! If the sleepies become yellow and slimy, it can point to a serious irritation or infection. Eye drops (from your vet) will quickly solve this problem. If the eyelid is infected, it can curl either inwards (entropion) or outwards (ectropion), depending on where the infection is.

Entropion and ectropion are not hereditary in cats, but the results of eye infections, which must not be ignored. Both the infected spot and the eyelashes can scratch the eyeball and thus damage the eye. Your vet needs to intervene as soon as possible to prevent further damage. Even already existing (slight) damage can be healed if a vet treats the condition on time.

Ears

The ears are often forgotten when looking after a cat, but they should be checked at least once a week. If your cat's ears are very dirty, or contain a lot of earwax, you need to clean them.

Preferably use a clean cotton cloth, moistened with some warm water or baby oil. Do not use cotton wool, because it can leave fluff behind. Never penetrate the ear canal with an object!

If you neglect cleaning your cat's ears, there's a serious risk of an ear infection. If your cat scratches

Eyes

You need to clean your cat's eyes once in a while. 'Sleepies' and bits of dry tear fluid can get stuck in the corners of the eyes. You can easily remove these by wiping them downwards with your thumb. If you don't like doing that, use a piece of tissue.

its ears a lot, or shakes its head, it might be suffering from dirty ears, an ear infection or ear mites (see the chapter "Parasites"). You then need to take it to the vet's.

Hairballs / eating grass

Every cat will clean itself thoroughly several times a day. Horny papillae make the tongue rough, which means hairs stick to the tongue easily and will then be swallowed. The Persian loses its long winter coat in the spring. You can help to remove dead hair by regularly brushing and combing your cat, but it will still swallow quite a bit of hair. All the swallowed hair gathers in the stomach and forms hairballs. At a certain moment, the cat will remove the hairball from its stomach by vomiting. The ball looks a bit like a wet, cigar-shaped mass of hair. Some of the hair will also leave the body by being excreted.

A cat that is allowed outdoors will regularly eat grass. The grass stimulates the stomach and causes the cat to expel the hair. A cat that is kept indoors needs to be given some grass once in a while. You can buy special bowls of cat grass in the pet shop for this purpose. You can also give your cat some special 'anti-hairball-paste', which causes the hairball to be expelled via the intestines.

Stud tail

Stud tail is a condition that develops through excess tail gland secretion on the upper surface of the tail. You can remove this skin fat by regularly putting talcum powder onto your cat's tail and brushing it out.

Cat grass

This condition is quite common amongst non-castrated tomcats under the influence of the hormone testosterone. It can, however, also occur in castrated tomcats or even in female cats.

There is not much point in washing your cat's tail, as fat does not dissolve in water. Washing your cat's tail with fat-dissolving shampoo does work, however. You need to rinse it very well! Some people come up with their own remedies. Maizena is put on some cats' tails (fat dissolves in fat), or even bran or other foods. It should be obvious that you should not even be tempted to start this.

Powdering the tail and brushing it out is a lot less messy, healthier for your cat, and also a lot more effective! If a lot of secretion is produced, some of the hair on your cat's tail may quickly stick together. It will be difficult to remove this lump. Do not, however, be tempted to cut it off, as the hair on the tail needs a long time to grow back.

Behaviour and upbringing

A cat is a very independent animal, which lives a solitary life. This means that cats do not naturally live in groups, and do not seem to like being subjected to a hierarchy.

However, in a group of cats, a pregnant or lactating cat seems to be the boss.

Its cheerful and inquisitive nature makes the Persian an ideal housemate. A cat is neither obedient nor disobedient, but just very self-willed. It is the small compromises and adjustments in the house that sweeten life with a cat. The Persian is affectionate and tolerant, and will try to avoid conflicts.

(Dis)obedience

When trying to teach a cat how to behave, or when trying to correct undesirable behaviour, you always need to be consistent. That means that your cat must never behave in a certain way, or may always

behave that way. Always reward your cat for good behaviour and tell it off with a strict voice for any wrongdoing. A plant spray is often used to reprimand a cat from a distance. You need to aim well, however, as cats can quickly jump aside, and you will end up having watered your furniture.

Try to ignore undesirable behaviour as far as possible. Your cat will perceive your reaction (even a negative one!) as a reward for its behaviour. Your voice is a very good tool to help you bring up your cat. It will either distract the cat, and thus draw its attention away from its mischief, or it will startle it, making it flee from the scene of its crime as quickly as possible.

House-training

Cats are very clean animals by nature. A lot of wild members of the cat family will use a stream to do their business in (if there's one available). Otherwise, excrement is buried. Litter boxes are very suitable inventions. As long as you keep your cat's litter box clean, it will readily make good use of it.

With newly born kittens, the mother licks their bellies so that excrement and urine are discharged. The mother will then lick it up. Once they reach approximately four or five weeks of age, kittens can control their own bowel motions. The young imitate their mother to a large extent, and the mother will also direct them towards the litter box. If a kitten ends up too far away from the litter box, it will huddle up whining at the skirting board. Carefully pick the kitten up and place it in the litter box.

What definitely does not work is to punish a kitten after an 'accident'. A kitten whose nose is rubbed in its urine or excrement will not understand what it did wrong, and it will only end up frightened of you. Also, punishing your cat next to the litter box, or a generally tense atmosphere, can cause (temporary) uncleanness, as the cat associates the litter box with something negative.

Litter box and cat litter

If you have just bought a cat or kitten, and it is your first or only cat, it makes sense to use the cat litter that the animal was used to at the breeder's or previous owner's home. If you already have a cat, which has been using a certain brand happily for a while, then keep on using this. The newcomer generally won't have too many problems with it.

There are many different brands and types of litter available in the shops. You can buy litter made of different types of basic material; there are products made of wood shavings, paper or clay (grit). They all have their advantages and disadvantages. Wood shavings and pressed paper are the most ecologically friendly and they are very light. This is an advantage when filling and cleaning the litter box. A disadvantage of it being so light is that it easily sticks to your cat's paws, fur and tail. This means that it will drop out of the fur somewhere 'en route', and you will then find plenty of litter in the area around the litter box.

Cat litter can make the surrounding air quite dusty. This depends on the brand of litter. The size of the individual kernels also makes a difference to some peoples' choice. Some believe that very fine litter sticks to the excrement better. You can buy very fine grit, which is almost like sand. You should choose the litter which best masks unpleasant smells and which is easiest to handle when you clean out the litter box (empty it). Which product you finally choose also depends on your cat's behaviour. A cat that does not bury its excrement always seems to produce more smell than a cat that does. In a group of cats, it might even be the case that only the cat highest in the hierarchy does not bury its excrement, as a reminder to the others about its position.

If your cat is unclean during the first few days in its new home, this might be the result of all the changes it is confronted with. Check the location of the litter box. It might be difficult for the cat to reach, or it might make the cat feel uncomfortable. You might find that changing the location of the litter box can provide the solution to your cat's uncleanness.

The litter box needs to be placed on a spot where your cat is given some privacy. It has to be placed in such a manner, however, that it can see another cat approaching, for example. Conflicts near your cat's litter box are often the cause of uncleanness. Also place the litter box where there is permanent shade. If the sun shines into the box, the warmth causes bacteria to reproduce quickly, and the smells that sometimes come from litter boxes are partly caused by bacteria.

Also have a good look at the type of litter box you bought. If you have a cat that enjoys digging, then it might be useful to buy a litter box with a door. This will be the most enclosed and will prevent the litter being spread everywhere. There are models with or without doors, with high or low sides, and with or without a lid. A lot of cats hate litter boxes with lids, as they have to sit in the lingering ammoniac fumes every time they want to do their business.

If you have another cat, it might bother the newcomer. Make sure that a cat sitting in the litter box can keep an eye on its environment. This way it can see a rival approaching and won't be frightened.

The unclean cat

If your cat decides to do its business next to its litter box, even if it has just been cleaned, there might be something wrong. If your cat excretes into the litter box, but urinates outside it, then it might be suffering from a bladder infection or bladder stones. If it urinates into the tray, but excretes next to it (or somewhere else), your cat might be suffering from intestinal irritation caused by worms, which leads to diarrhoea.

Some cats prefer to use two litter boxes, one for excrement and one for urine. If your cat does its business outside the litter box, and you think that its recuperation might take some time, put a doormat on the spot the cat has chosen. It is easy to clean, dries quickly and prevents unpleasant smells developing.

Play and toys

Playing is very important to cats. In the wild, kittens play with their siblings, and thus practise the behaviour they need for later life. Play is also very important as physical exercise and as interaction between man and cat.

Some cats have the tendency to bite into things. A ball of wool is therefore not a very suitable toy for a cat, as it can ingest a string of wool or choke on it, with all the horrific consequences. Cats can also ingest wrapping string.

They also love playing with balls made of aluminium foil, but if a cat bites into such as ball, it can swallow small pieces, so do not offer these as toys. Proper balls are great toys, and your pet shop will have a wide assortment of toys that have been made especially for cats. Persians often enjoy retrieving things.

Aggression and fear

Cats are very rarely aggressive towards people. As with all animals, aggressive behaviour is usually caused by the human behaving wrongly. In human terms, cats sometimes seem very aggressive towards each other, although this hardly ever results in serious injuries.

A cat might be distant towards people. The reason for this behaviour is usually to be found in the first few weeks of a cat's life. A lack of new experiences during this important phase (which is called the 'socialisation phase') has a huge influence on a cat's behaviour in later life. A cat that never encountered humans, other cats or other animals during the socialisation phase will be scared of them later. This fear is common with cats that grew up in barns, cellars or attics, without sufficient human contact. It is very important for a cat to get as many new impressions as possible during its first few weeks.

There are some well known situations in which cats are scared, the most common are thunderstorms and fireworks. If your cat is very scared of fireworks, you can ask the vet for some tranquillisers or homeopathic remedies.

Some people put their cat in the bathroom on Guy Fawkes Night or New Year's Eve. If the bathroom is fairly central in the house, the cat will have fewer problems with the noise. If your cat has some negative memories of the bathroom, find a different room. Or draw the blinds in another room, which you think is the most suitable as a 'safe place' for your cat.

Try to behave as normally as possible. Your cat will probably find it all a lot less scary if you show it that nothing is bothering you. Make sure, however, that your cat stays indoors. If your cat is outdoors when the fireworks start, it might panic, which may cause it to run away, and it might actually not find its way home again.

Meowing

Some cats meow more than others. Some owners believe that their cats are very 'talkative'. Meowing can be an attempt to get the owner's attention. If a kitten has just moved home, it will meow for its mother and siblings. There are different intonations in meows, depending on their purpose. When a kitten calls for its lost family, this is the right moment to call it by its name. When it meows, it is seeking contact, which you can then take advantage of. Some cats meow when they are about to get fed, or when you surprise them with a tasty treat.

Both female and male cats will be quite vocal during puberty. Tomcats will run through the house meowing loudly, so that all the female cats in the area know of their presence. When a female cat comes into season for the first time, she meows and screams in all sorts of intonations in order to let all the tomcats in the neighbourhood know that she is ready to mate. Do not mistake your cat's heat for some rare disease, as she isn't really in pain, even if it may seem like it.

Undesirable behaviour

Any cat can display undesirable behaviour. You will not succeed in teaching your cat tricks, but it will understand real prohibitions, such as not jumping on the table or the bed; quite often only when you are near, though. Be on the safe side in any case. A cooker with soft-touch buttons can be activated by your cat walking over it. Make sure that you can switch the appliance off completely (not just put it on stand-by).

Most people are not keen on their cat scratching at furniture. Make sure that your cat has its own scratching pole or plank. A cat that is only kept in the house can show more of a tendency to scratch at things. A cat that is allowed outdoors will sharpen its nails on shrubs and trees.

Protect your computer from your cat, or place it in a locked room or a cupboard. Accidents (such as your cat vomiting on the keyboard) are just waiting to happen. Young, spraying, tomcats have also caused a lot of computer nightmares.

Breeding

Reproduction is a very important part of a cat's natural behaviour. Your happy little kitten will eventually become an adult cat and its instincts will make themselves heard. This is great for people who like breeding cats.

Those who just want a 'cosy companion' however will miss the regular adventures with females on heat and calling males like a hole in the head. Even if you do not intend to breed cats, it is still important to know a little about reproduction among cats, so that you understand why your cat behaves in a certain way, and what you can do about this behaviour.

To breed or not to breed...
You need to decide whether or not you want to breed with your female Persian (even if it is to be just once) before you buy her. If you intend to breed cats later on, it will have an influence on the kitten you choose. You need to ensure that you will end up with healthy, pretty youngsters, but

you also need to take your available time, financial situation and your dedication into account. Time and space are pretty self-explanatory. As far as costs are concerned, they can be quite high: medical tests, some of which are mandatory and some of which you might choose to have done, the covering fee, getting registration as a cattery, plenty of equipment for the birth, and medical costs if any kittens become ill.

Dedication goes further than thinking that problems are all explained in books and that they always happen to other people anyway. Kittens might die and you need to be absolutely certain that you can deal with that emotionally.

You need to socialise the kittens: you have to get them used to strangers, unusual noises, but also to everyday things, such as the vacuum cleaner, the steam cleaner, or the egg timer. You also need to get young Persians used to being thoroughly combed, brushed and even bathed from the age of 6 weeks. When trying to find new homes for your kittens, it helps if you are a good judge of human nature. Of course, you want to make sure that the kittens find a new owner that suits them. In short, there's a lot you need to do if you want to breed a litter of kittens.

Liability
Breeding cats is much more than simply 1+1= many. If you're planning to breed with your Persian, be on your guard. The whole affair can quite easily turn into a financial disaster, because, under the law, a breeder is liable for the 'quality' of his kittens.

A good breeder will place strict demands on the animals he wants to use for breeding. They need to be checked for certain hereditary abnormalities. By fulfilling these criteria, the breeder shows his sense of responsibility. If you breed a litter of kittens and sell them without the proper checks having been made, you can be held liable by the new owners for any costs arising from any inherited defects that might turn up in later life. These (veterinary)

costs can be enormous! So contact a breed association if you plan to breed a litter of Persians. Find out all the relevant information about which medical tests are mandatory and which are advisable.

Keeping a stud
It is not advisable to keep a stud in the house. He will follow his instincts, i.e. spray urine all over the house, and sharp reprimands will certainly not help to stop this behaviour. A stud will spray anything and everything, including your furniture, house plants, walls, your bed, your children's school bags, your books, etc.

You will need to build a stud house for your stud. Your neighbours, however, might not be too happy about that. Not only will the stud meow quite loudly, but he will also spray his surroundings. Good cleaning is therefore a must. The stud house will also need to be frost-proof in the winter. Simply knocking together a wooden hut will not be enough. Both the breeding associations and the law provide rules for suitable accommodation. Stick to minimum sizes, headroom and other requirements. They have all been made to ensure the well-being of the animal.

A stud will also have queens (as female cats for breeding are called) in for mating from time to time. At the end of a mating session, the queen will scream. This can wake

up your neighbours. If your stud never has any queens in for mating, it is best to have him castrated and let him have a place on your couch. You will also have to constantly advertise your stud and/or show him off at cat shows.

The female on heat

From about six months onwards, a female cat will come on heat. An adolescent cat's first season does not normally last all that long. The length of a normal season can vary from a few days to two weeks. Note the length of her seasons in a diary if you intend to breed with your female. A female that is only on heat for a very short time will need to go to the stud a lot quicker than one that has a longer season. A female cat will not lose blood when it is in season like a female dog, for example. She will clean her vulva a lot, and will nudge everyone and everything in her area with her head. She might even try to entice the family dog, which will certainly not know what is going on. The cat will go down on her front legs, put her tail to the side and push her genitalia up.

A female cat will be too young to be covered during her first season, but she must still be kept indoors. You must not even let her out in the garden, as tomcats will always find a female on heat wherever she is. When your cat is twelve to eighteen months old, she is old enough to be covered. Besides her physical maturity, you also need to bear in mind your cat's mental maturity.

It is usual in the cat breeding world that mating takes place at the stud's place. Whether the stud lives close by or far away, you still need to bring your cat to him by car. Even a short trip in the car can affect a female cat so much that she no longer seems on heat when she arrives at the stud's home. You will not be the first to desperately try to explain that your cat was very much in season when you left home. Just give her some time. The stud's owner, too, will be able to reassure you. Your cat's heat will return later that day or on the following day, and stud and queen will be ready to be put together for mating. The queen's ovulation is stimulated by the actual covering. One mating session is normally enough, but to avoid unnecessary travelling and further mating attempts, you should leave queen and stud together for a further one or two days after the first successful covering.

Most female cats are on heat a few times a year. Some females come on heat every three weeks, but have longer intervals between 'serious' heats. The time of year has an influence on the female cat's cycle, but some cats seem to have a biorhythm of their own. By noting your female cat's seasons in a diary, or on a spare page in her passport, you will almost certainly be able to determine her rhythm over the years.

A female on heat will eat very little. If a cat comes on heat too often, she will become very thin, which in turn is detrimental to her health. A female that is on heat too often will also often not become pregnant after being covered. Cysts are often the cause of this problem.

If you do plan to breed with your Persian in the future, sterilisation is obviously not an option to prevent unwanted offspring in the meantime. A contraceptive pill can be a temporary solution, although it is not all that wise to use hormonal medication on animals intended for breeding. The contraceptive pill is also blamed for causing serious side effects, such as uteritis.

Phantom pregnancy

Phantom pregnancies do sometimes occur in cats, but usually only after they have been covered. Look at your cat's teats approximately 19 to 21 days after the mating. If they are slightly swollen and pinkish, then you can assume that she is pregnant. In the case of a phantom pregnancy, the teats will also swell up, just as in a normal pregnancy. However, this swelling will usually occur approximately nine weeks after the mating, when the cat would normally be giving birth. Many

owners then expect their cat to give birth, right up to the very last possible moment. If nothing happens, the vet will often diagnose a phantom pregnancy. The milk production will eventually stop by itself, but to prevent further problems, the vet will usually intervene with a regulating injection.

The female will usually come into season again approximately seven weeks after an unsuccessful covering. Her body had been preparing for giving birth. It is best to ignore this season to give the female's hormone levels time to stabilise and prepare for a new season and pregnancy. Some cats, however, seem unable to ever become pregnant and give birth. If your cat has gone through several phantom pregnancies, it is best to have her sterilised.

Homeopathic medication can help in dealing with phantom pregnancies. It might be necessary, however, to administer hormonal treatment over a short period of time. If the teats are heavily swollen, gently rubbing them with camphor spirit can give relief. Gently rubbing them with ice cubes or a cold cloth (moisten and freeze) can also help against the pain.

Preparations for breeding a litter

If you do plan to breed a litter of kittens, you need to wait until your cat is physically and mentally fully grown before you have her covered.

If your cat is a purebred Persian, then it makes sense to mate her with the best possible candidate. Always be meticulous with your preparations. You also need to bear in mind that accompanying your cat through pregnancy, birth and the first twelve weeks afterwards is a time-consuming affair. Never breed with cats that have hereditary abnormalities. The same applies to cats with a less than desirable character. A very shy cat will not only pass on her fear genetically, but her kittens will also imitate her behaviour. If, while she lies suckling her kittens, the cat ducks down as soon as she hears the vacuum cleaner, the doorbell or a child coming home from school, the kittens will feel this and take on their mother's fears.

If your Persian has a pedigree, then mate her with a stud that also has one. For more information about breeding cats, you can contact the breed associations or the breeder you bought your cat from. Before having your cat covered, treat her against worms with a wormer.

The owner of the stud might require you to have your cat's health checked. These tests are normally done to exclude the possibility of the stud becoming infected by deadly viruses. The biggest concerns are normally Feline Leukaemia Virus (FeLV) and Feline Aids (Feline Immunodeficiency Virus). Your vet will take some blood from your cat and do the tests, sometimes sending the blood to a laboratory. You will receive a written result, which you can hand to the owner of the stud.

It is, of course, tempting to choose the stud with the most prizes and titles, especially if he lives in the neighbourhood. Breeding, however, is intended to improve the breed and conserve it as well as possible. To keep a population healthy, it is important to ensure a genetic variety (i.e. mating animals with different genetic dispositions). Not every cat owner goes to shows, which means that, if you just look at show results, you might miss the perfect partner for your cat, just because he does not have a show career.

Pregnancy

It is difficult to determine at first whether or not your cat is pregnant. Only after about four to five weeks will her belly become noticeably larger. If you want to be absolutely certain that your cat is pregnant, you can ask the vet to do an ultrasound scan.

During the last few weeks of pregnancy, a cat's behaviour will change noticeably, and her teats will swell up. An average pregnancy lasts 63 days and will cost the cat a lot of energy. At the beginning of the pregnancy, you should feed your cat her normal amount of food. During the further course of the pregnancy, however, your cat's nutritional needs will increase in leaps and bounds. It will now be ideal to feed her with dry food, as you can leave some out for her throughout the day. The pregnant female will control her diet herself, as cats generally only eat what they really need.

If your cat only eats canned food, then feed her a little more than normal. She will tell you when she needs more. The mother-to-be will have an increased demand for energy and proteins in the last phase of the pregnancy. During the last few weeks of the pregnancy, you can feed your cat a concentrated high-energy food (such as dry kitten food). Feed canned food in several portions a day, as your cat will no longer be able to deal with large amounts of food at once.

After approximately seven weeks, your cat will display nesting behaviour: she will look for a place to give birth to her young. The birthing box needs to be available at least a week before the birth, so that she can get used to it. Put the birthing box in a quiet, draught-free, secluded spot, which still allows the mother-to-be to keep an eye on her surroundings.

Never give a pregnant cat medicines or wormers, as some products can be dangerous to the unborn kittens. An exception is, of course, an emergency that really endangers the cat's health. Your vet will then be able to decide which medication is the most appropriate.

The birth

The mother-to-be will become restless one to two days before the birth. She will start digging around in all the old towels and newspapers which you put into the birthing box. She might have some slimy discharge without blood. The birth will then normally start within the next 24 hours. Phone your vet to let him know that the birth is imminent, so that you can quickly get help from the right address or a suitable replacement, even in the middle of the night or at the weekend.

Once the first contractions have started, the first kittens will

Golden tabby kitten

your cat seems calm and fairly comfortable, let her have these rests. If she gets anxious, however, and the contractions start without any kittens being born, then you should ask your vet to come and have a look. A labour-inducing injection is often the solution. Once the birth is over, you need to be able to count as many after-births as kittens. If this is not the case, contact your vet. An injection is normally sufficient to remove the last after-birth from the womb.

Suckling

After the birth, the mother's milk production will start. Lactation demands a lot from a cat. During the first three to four weeks, the kittens are totally dependent on their mother's milk. The mother will require extra food and fluids during this period. This can be up to three or four times the normal amount. If the mother produces too little milk, you can supplement it by bottle-feeding the kittens with special kitten milk.

normally appear within an hour. The best ambient temperature for the birth is 25 °C. Kittens are wet when they are born, and the change from the mother's warm body to a surrounding temperature of, say, 18 °C, is a bit too abrupt. Remain calm and talk to your cat in a soothing voice. While they are still in the uterus, the kittens are supplied with oxygen via the umbilical cord. As soon as they are born, they will need to use their lungs. A newly born kitten is still in the amnion. If the mother does not react immediately by licking off the amnion, then you must intervene and remove it, otherwise the kitten will suffocate.

The kittens are usually born in intervals of forty-five minutes. The mother might have breaks in-between, so the whole affair can easily take a few hours. As long as

It is best to divide the large amount of food your cat needs into several smaller portions. Here too, choose a concentrated high-energy food. Make sure your cat has plenty of fresh drinking water. Do not feed her cow's milk, however, as this can cause diarrhoea.

It is important to keep a good eye on your cat at this stage. Uteritis can develop if an after-birth or a

dead kitten has remained in the uterus, or even after excessive pressing. The cat will be less interested in her kittens, and she may have fever and a brown discharge. Your vet will need to help here. Also check her teats every day, as one or more of them could become inflamed. This is very painful for the cat. An inflamed teat will feel hard, swollen and hot. A few days before the birth, your cat will be quite willing to let you near her belly. This is the right moment to carefully shorten the hair around her teats. If milk gets into the long hair, it can make it stick together and cover the teats, making it impossible for the kittens to drink.

Another problem that can occur is eclampsia. A calcium shortage in the blood will cause muscle cramps, excessive salivation and dilated pupils. You must not confuse this with the enlarged pupils a cat has when sitting in a dark spot, as they are then naturally dilated. Never think that eclampsia will go away by itself, because it won't. Your cat could even die if you do not intervene in time. Your vet can help and stop this condition quickly with a calcium injection. If your Persian has a large litter, keep a particularly watchful eye on her with regard to eclampsia.

Weaning

You can start feeding the kittens some solid food when they are approximately three to four weeks old. There are special kitten foods available, which follow on well from the mother's milk, and which are easy for the kittens to chew with their milk teeth.

Ideally, kittens should be weaned at an age of ten to twelve weeks, as they no longer need to rely on their mother's milk at this age. The mother's milk production will slowly stop and her nutritional needs will also return to normal. Within a few weeks after weaning, your cat should again be getting the same amount of food as before the pregnancy.

Castration and sterilisation

If you are really sure that your cat should never have a(nother) litter, then it is best to have her sterilised. During sterilisation (which is actually the same as castration) the ovaries, and often also the uterus, are removed in an operation. Your cat will no longer come into season, and cannot become pregnant. The best time for sterilisation is when a cat is approximately ten months old, as she is then more or less fully grown.

A tomcat is usually castrated to prevent unwanted sexual behaviour. During castration, the testicles are removed. Problems are very rarely encountered during this simple operation. A tomcat is normally castrated when he is approximately nine months old.

Silver classic tabby

Shows

When you went to see your cat's breeder, you probably saw a lot of colourful rosettes hanging on the walls and a number of shining trophies on a sideboard. On your kitten's pedigrees, some of the names probably have pretty respectable titles next to them.

In your opinion, your Persian is probably the most beautiful and most lovable cat in the world. You might, however, want to know what a judge would make of it, in which case you need to enter it in a cat show.

Visiting a show should be a pleasurable experience for both owner and cat. For some cat lovers it is an intensive hobby and they visit numerous shows every year. Others find it nice to visit an exemption show with their cat just once. Visiting a cat show is worth it for anyone: an experienced judge will look at your Persian and judge it according to its appearance and condition. His report will show you your cat's strong and weak points, and this could help you

when looking for a mate for breeding, for example. During a show, you can also swap experiences with other owners of Persians. Of course, it is great if you think that going to cat shows is good fun, but the priority must always be that your cat enjoys it too. Only ever take your pets to shows if they enjoy it themselves. Too much stress can make a cat more receptive to viruses and bacteria.

About shows
The National Cat Club was formed in the UK in 1887. It joined hands with another organisation in 1910 and the Governing Council of the Cat Fancy was a created. In 1983 a new club, the Cat Association of Britain, was set up.

Different cat clubs have their own lists of recognised breeds and official standards.

The world's largest cat show is organised under GCCF rules. The National Cat club started this event in 1887. All 2000 entries are judged in one open class or breed class. This show knows no Best in Show reward or Supreme award. When your cat has won several open breed classes at previous shows it's allowed to enter GCCF's Supreme show.

In case you want to enter a show it's necessary to have your cat properly registered.
Some associations have facilities for non-pedigree cats to be registered. These cats can get fancy titles like: Master, Grand Master, CA Champion, CA Grand Pet, CA Supreme Pet.

When you have decided to enter a show you need to get registration information from the organising association. The internet is quite useful in this matter. A few days prior to the show you will receive all necessary documents.

Ring shows
The CA organises the judging in 'rings' in which each 'ring' seems to have its own show. Like this it's worth the money for the audience and exhibitors don't need to travel to many shows. At

'ring' shows exhibitors can put their cats in colourfully fitted out show cages. Judges can't see all this fancy stuff, as stewards bring the cats to the judges in the ring.

Blue classic tabby

Red tabby point

It all depends on the show ruling whether an official report is written, a verbal critique is given or if just a point form is written.

On-Floor judging

In this case the cats sit and wait in a numbered pen, which is only fitted out with a white blanket, white litter tray and water bowl. Each judge is accompanied by a steward. The steward takes each cat out of its cage to assess it. The judge places the exhibits and official prize slips will be posted on an award board.

At some shows ribbons or rosettes are placed on the show cages. A playful and colourful event for happy exhibitors!

Getting ready for the show

Obviously, your cat needs to be in perfect condition for the show. A judge will not be impressed if its coat is not clean or is tangled, and if there are remains of soil, sand or twigs in it. Its nails must be clipped and its teeth must be free of tartar. Showing cats is actually more like a beauty pageant. Your cat also needs to be free of any parasites and illnesses. Its coat must be impeccable and eyes and ears must be spotlessly clean. If you only start with this a few days before the show, you will definitely be too late. To achieve the best results, you need to keep your cat in peak condition all the time. This does not mean just brushing your cat once in a while, but also checking its eyes and ears and cleaning them if necessary.

Wash your Persian approximately a week before the cat show, as it will then look at its best. Your cat's coat will be in top condition if it is brushed regularly. A Persian with a showing career ahead of it will need to be trimmed quite regularly. This is both to get it used to it, but also to keep it looking its best. There are a lot of things you need to be aware of when getting your Persian ready for a show. It would take up too much space to try and explain the whole process here. It is best to go and watch (and help) an experienced exhibitor prepare his animals. If you do not have anybody suitable in your area, invest some money and have your cat prepared at a grooming parlour. You will be able to do it yourself before the next show.

While a female on heat is actually allowed at shows, the other competitors will not be too happy about her presence. Her moaning and the calls of excited tomcats can cause irritation in animals and owners.

Your cat must also not exhibit any physical abnormalities. A bent tail, an undershot jaw (lower jaw protrudes over upper jaw) or an overshot jaw (upper jaw protrudes over lower jaw) are not allowed at shows. A tomcat must be in possession of both testicles.

Do not forget!

If you plan to go to a show with your cat, you need to be well prepared. Do not forget any of the following items:

For yourself:
- Registration card
- Food and drink
- Folding chair

For your cat:
- Cat passport
- Registration card
- Litter box
- Cat litter
- Food and drink bowls
- Food
- Curtains for the cage
- Blanket or cushion
- Comb and brush
- Talcum powder

the **Persian cat**

Parasites

All cats are vulnerable to various sorts of parasites. Parasites are minute creatures, which live at the expense of their host animals. They feed on blood, flakes of skin and other bodily substances. There are two main types of parasites.

External parasites, such as fleas and ticks, live in the cat's coat. Cats can also suffer from ear mites, which live in the ear. Ringworm can also be found on cats. Internal parasites, such as tapeworms and roundworms, live in their host's body.

Fleas

Fleas feed on a cat's blood. They cause not only itching and skin problems, but can also carry infections, such as tapeworm. In large numbers, they can cause anaemia and cats can also become allergic to a flea's saliva (flea allergy), which can cause serious skin conditions.

So it's important that you treat your cat for fleas as effectively as possible. Do not just treat the animal itself, but also its surroundings. There are various medicines to treat your cat: drops for the neck and to put in its food, flea collars, long-life sprays and flea powders. There are various sprays in pet shops, which can be used to eradicate fleas in the cat's immediate surroundings. Choose a spray that kills both adult fleas and their larvae. If your cat goes in your car, you should spray that too.

Fleas can also affect other pets, so you should treat those too. When spraying a room, cover any aquarium or fishbowl. If the spray reaches the water it will be fatal for your fish! Switch off the oxygen pump for an hour or so. During and just after the spraying, you should not let your pets into the room. Wear a mask or use a scarf to cover your nose and mouth.

Your vet and pet shop have a wide range of flea treatments and can advise you on the subject. Always follow the instructions on the packaging closely. Change the brand once in a while, as parasites can build up a resistance to certain products. This means that a product might be less effective after some time. Different products have different active ingredients.

Ticks

Ticks are small, spider-like insects. They live in shrubs, long grass, parks and woods, but possibly also in your own back garden. A cat allowed outdoors could go through infested shrubs. The ticks will then drop onto the cat here. Ticks feed on their victims' blood. A tick looks like a small, grey leather bag with eight feet. When a tick is full, it can be five to ten times its original size and darker in colour.

Ticks do not just cause irritation by their blood-sucking, but they can also transmit a number of nasty diseases. If you repeatedly find ticks on your outdoor cat, then an anti-tick collar can be a good solution. An anti-tick/anti-flea collar does not prevent the tick attaching to the cat, but it will prevent it enjoying its meal.

Infections occur when the tick has almost finished its meal and the collar prevents this happening. Removing a tick is easy with tick tweezers. Grip the tick with the tweezers, as close to the cat's skin as possible, and carefully pull it out with a turning movement. You must disinfect the spot where the tick had been with iodine to prevent infection. It is a bad idea to 'numb' a tick by covering it in alcohol, ether or oil. In a shock reaction, the tick may discharge the infected contents of its stomach into your cat's skin. It is important to fight ticks as effectively as possible. Check your cat regularly, especially if it runs around a lot in woods and shrubs.

Tick

Lyme disease is becoming increasingly common here. If you have been bitten by a tick, go to your GP immediately. Timely treatment can prevent a lot of problems later. If you have been infected with Lyme disease, you will develop a red patch around the tick's bite within a few days. You will also have flu-like symptoms, which can then develop into fever, swollen joints, loss of appetite and even acute paralysis. Your cat will not be happy if you are ill!

Ear mite

The ear mite is the most common mite, and it can be found in the cat's ears. If you check your cat's

Red with white,
blue

ears every week, you will spot a waxy, brown discharge from its ears if it is infected with ear mites. An infected cat will also shake its head a lot and scratch its ears.

Mites can sit quite deep in the ear canal. Just cleaning the auricle with some cotton wool is not sufficient. Never fumble around in your cat's ears with a cotton bud. You could seriously damage something and simply cleaning its ears doesn't help anyway. Your vet will be able to prescribe an anti-mite ointment. Ear mites can be quite resilient. Take your cat to the vet's regularly for check-ups. Ear mites can easily be passed on to other cats, but also to dogs (and vice versa).

Ringworm

Any cat can be infected by ringworm, although it seems that we hear of it more often with Persians. The reason for this might be that the long hair covers up the condition in the first phase. It is therefore not spotted as quickly as with other cats.

The name 'ringworm' probably makes you think that this is a worm, but it is actually a fungus. Typical symptoms of ringworm are red, round, bald patches. The patches are round, because this is the way the fungus spreads. These patches are usually found around the head and ears, but also on the back, the front paws and at the nails.

If the condition is not diagnosed quickly, then scabs can develop, which are sometimes scaly. Your vet can do a test, or look at the patches under a special (ultraviolet) lamp. If the patches are small, the fungus will normally be easy to stop. If you have several cats at home, then some of them might be carriers. In this case they can be infected without displaying any symptoms. They can, however, pass on the disease. Ringworm can also be passed on between humans and cats. You can infect your cat and vice versa, and a cat can also infect a dog. Treatment on humans generally consists of treatment with an ointment. It is a very intensive treatment. All your cats (and other pets) also need to be treated. Your cats (and other pets) need to be washed with a special shampoo twice a week. You will need to carry on this treatment until all the patches have vanished. To totally eradicate the fungus, it as absolutely vital to also treat the surroundings.

To prevent the spread of diseases, it is important not to let animals with ear mites or ringworm change owners.

Worms

Cats can suffer from various types of worm. The most common are tapeworm and roundworm. Tapeworm eggs are often transmitted by fleas. The cat becomes infected by swallowing a flea that carries the disease. Tapeworms live in the intestines and can cause diarrhoea and poor condition. You might find segments of the worm (which look like rice kernels) around your cat's anus, in its breech (the long hairs on the back legs) and on its bed. It is then absolutely vital to treat your cat with a wormer. You will also need to treat the cat and its surroundings against fleas.

Roundworms are parasites that regularly return. They cause diarrhoea and loss of weight, and they can disturb the growth of kittens. Kittens are often infected via their mother's milk. A kitten can lose weight, but have a swollen belly. The worms are sometimes visible when the cat vomits. They look like spaghetti-like tendrils. They are also visible in its excrement. A kitten needs to be wormed regularly in its first year. You can use the following worming plan: at two, four, six, eight, sixteen, twenty-four weeks and then after three months. Grown cats need to be treated against worms twice a year.

Roundworms

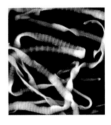

Tapeworms

Your Persian's health

There is not enough space in this book to deal with all the medical ups and downs of the Persian. We will, however, go into some of the illnesses that you might encounter.

Cream

Some hereditary disorders can be eradicated from a breed, some faster than others. The best way to gain control over such problems is to encourage breeders and owners to be open about any hereditary abnormalities they might find in their animals. At present, the population of Persians in the UK is not particularly affected by hereditary problems. The Persian is a healthy cat, but, as any other breed, it can be affected by viruses, for example. This is why we focus on two viral diseases in this chapter: Feline Panleukopenia and Cat Flu. They are the most common illnesses with cats. Cats should be vaccinated against these diseases once a year. There are also other well known virus diseases, such as Feline Leukaemia, Feline Aids (Feline Immunodeficiency

Virus, FIV), and FIP (Feline Infectious Peritonitis). In the wet form of FIP, a large accumulation of fluid develops in the abdominal cavity. In the dry form, the FIP virus can settle in any organ, depending on each individual case: an animal with FIP in the brain will show neurological disorders. If the virus settles in the liver, a yellow colouring will appear in the mucous membranes as a sign that something is wrong with the liver. But not every brain or liver abnormality is caused by FIP. Cat Leukaemia is not at all related to Leukaemia as we know it from human medicine. It also cannot be transferred from cat to man or vice versa. Feline Aids can also not be transferred from animal to human. Characteristic of these three virus diseases is that they are fatal. A post mortem will often reveal whether one of these diseases was the cause of death. In veterinary forensic science, Leukaemia is given an incubation period of 53 days in animals younger than two years. Feline Aids is given two weeks and FIP four months.

Feline Panleukopenia

The cause of this disease is a Parvovirus, which was first recorded in 1928. Our feline population is quite well protected by regular vaccinations. Animals lacking immunisation can easily contract this disease, however. The course of the disease can be so acute that it looks like a case of poisoning. In the case of such a quick progression, the syndrome does not normally develop completely; another reason to think of something else as the cause of death. Kittens which have not yet had their vaccination belong to the risk group.

The first symptoms are weakness, apathy and lack of appetite. The body temperature rises very quickly. After a few days, the temperature drops, only to rise again the following day. This last symptom also occurs with FIP (Feline Infectious Peritonitis). At this stage, the cat typically vomits semi-digested food, but also white and yellow (gall) slime. Liquid diarrhoea follows, which smells extremely bad. This is caused by serious damage to the intestinal

mucous membrane. The animals dehydrate very quickly due to the excessive loss of body fluids (through vomiting and diarrhoea). They also lose weight very quickly. The loss of fluids is not compensated by drinking. The cat might be standing with its head over its water bowl and not actually drink anything. With many diseases, not all symptoms occur in all patients. Not all cats with Panleukopenia will vomit, for example. The virus can be found in vomit, urine, diarrhoea, blood, saliva and tear fluid. It is thus very important to disinfect everything very well. Ask your vet for advice. Note: The incubation period is 3 to 9 days.

Cat Flu

Cat Flu is a term used very often. Almost all illnesses that come with sneezing and infected eyes and mucous membranes (in the mouth and nose) are given the name Cat Flu. Cat Flu is caused by Feline Viral Rhinotracheitis or a Calicivirus. In the first case, we are dealing with a disorder of the respiratory tract, caused by the Feline Rhinotracheitis Herpes Virus.

As the name indicates, this disease is accompanied by sneezing. This can vary from a very mild to a very serious degree. Even only slight sneezing complaints can develop into serious discharge from the nose, combined with continuous sneezing fits, the development of crusts around nose and eyes and swollen mucous membranes in the eyes, nose and mouth. If its nose is blocked, your cat will soon stop eating, as a cat will only eat what it can smell. Make sure you offer your cat food with a strong smell, and if necessary you might even have to force-feed your cat (liquid food can be a solution). In the case of the Calicivirus, the cat displays physical abnormalities, it seems to be paralysed, which is normally over within two to four days.

It is important to have your cat treated by the vet if it is suffering from Cat Flu. Antibiotics do not work against viruses, but they will help to prevent secondary infections.

Kittens can be very receptive to this disease, especially in the period when the antibodies they received from their mother lose their effect. The vaccination itself can cause a vaccination reaction. With cats, stress often causes viruses to attack, which can eventually cause Cat Flu. A visit to the vet's or to a cat show, the arrival of a new cat in your home, leaving the nest and especially having to get used to a new home are all high-stress situations for cats. You can compare it to children in a school class, who all infect each other. If your recently bought kitten starts sneezing, even though it seemed fine so far, it does not necessarily mean that you bought a sick animal. Try to avoid stress as much as possible, for example, do not let all the kids from the neighbourhood come and admire your new housemate.
Note: The incubation time is one to two days.

Runny eyes

The more extreme your Persian's head shape is, the more chance there is of an abnormality of the tear ducts. Your Persian might develop ocular discharge – brown-yellow wet discharge under the corners of the eyes. If your Persian is light coloured, its coat might become discoloured. Depending on how badly your cat's eyes water, you will need to clean them often or very often. Pet shops have special products for cleaning your cat's eyes.

In general

If a relatively new or even (at first sight) unknown condition develops in your cat, a post mortem can be very helpful to find out more after the animal's death. Send the results to the breed club and your cat's breeder, so that they can check out and process these. You can ask for a cosmetic autopsy if you want your pet to be buried or cremated in a respectable state.

Colourpoint Persians have blue eyes

Useful addresses

www.pedigreecat.co.uk
These pages are dedicated to pedigree cats in the UK. The site contains photographs and information about the different breeds of cats that are currently available in Great Britain. There are also links to cat breeders, registering organizations and other cat related sites.

www.cats-dogs.co.uk
Provides a quick route to finding the services you require for your cats. Finds catteries, boarding kennels, veterinary surgeons or other pet services & supplies.

www.catsnkittens.co.uk
This site is full of information on Britain's most popular pet. Breeders, advice, kittens for sale, studs, clubs & societies, boarding catteries, shows and much more!

www.petplanet.co.uk
Find information on dogs, cats and pets here. You'll find breed profiles of dogs and cats or your nearest vets, kennels, catteries or breeds societies. Visit Pet Talk and ask for advice about specific breeds, or share stories about dogs and cats with our thousands of regular visiting pet lovers.

Useful addresses

The Governing Council of the Cat Fancy or GCCF
4 - 6 Penel Orlieu
Bridgwater, Somerset
TA6 3PG, UK
Tel: +44 (0)1278 427575
Website:
http://ourworld.compuserve.com/homepages/GCCF_CATS/index.htm
email: info@gccfcats.org

Cat Clubs
A Directory of Cat Clubs and Societies
This directory lists some of the many breed societies and area cat clubs in the British Isles.
http://members.aol.com/cattrust/catclubs.htm

Cat Club Northern Ireland
Catclub.net
8 Deramore Gardens
Belfast , N. Ireland
BT7 3FN
Tel: (028) 90597251
e-mail: charlotte@catclub.net
www.catclub.net/home.cfm

Persian Blue Cat Society
Email:
bpcs@bluepersian.ndirect.co.uk
Website:
www.bluepersian.ndirect.co.uk

About Pets

- The Border Collie
- The Boxer
- The Bulldog
- The Cavalier King Charles Spaniel
- The Cocker Spaniel
- The Dalmatian
- The Dobermann
- The English Springer Spaniel
- The German Shepherd
- The Golden Retriever
- The Jack Russell Terrier
- The Labrador Retriever
- The Puppy
- The Rottweiler
- The Siberian Husky
- The Shih Tzu
- The Stafforshire Bull Terrier
- The Yorkshire Terrier
- The African Grey Parrot
- The Canary
- The Budgerigar
- The Cockatiel
- The Finches
- The Lovebird
- The Parrot
- The Kitten
- The Cat
- The Siamese cats
- The Persian cat
- The Chipmunk
- The Dwarf Hamster
- The Dwarf Rabbit
- The Ferret
- The Gerbil
- The Guinea Pig
- The Hamster
- The Mouse
- The Rabbit
- The Rat
- The Goldfish
- The Tropical Fish
- The Snake
- The Tortoise

about pets

Key features of the series are:
- Most affordable books
- Packed with hands-on information
- Well written by experts
- Easy to understand language
- Full colour original photography
- 70 to 110 photos
- All one needs to know to care well for one's pet
- Trusted authors, veterinary consultants, breed and species expert authorities
- Appropriate for first time pet owners
- Interesting detailed information for pet professionals
- Title range includes books for advanced pet owners and breeders
- Includes useful addresses, veterinary data, breed standards.

The Persian cat

Country of origin:	Iran / Great Britain
Other name:	Longhair
Weight:	2.8 – 6 kg
Colour:	Basically any possible colour
Coat:	Long with undercoat
Character:	Affectionate, patient, sensitive, individualistic, intelligent, compliant, easy-going, curious, quiet, friendly, good-natured
Life expectancy:	12 – 15 years

the **Persian cat**